The Ultimate Business Planner for Thriving Enterprises

"Strategies, Tools, and Insights to Navigate Your Path to Prosperity"

Kitchen Mage

The target audience

1. Entrepreneurs: Seeking comprehensive guidance to launch and grow their ventures.
2. Small Business Owners: Looking for practical tools and strategies to streamline operations and boost profitability.
3. Startups: Needing a roadmap to navigate the challenges of early-stage growth and scale sustainably.
4. Corporate Executives: Seeking innovative approaches to drive organizational success and achieve strategic goals.
5. Solopreneurs: Wanting tailored solutions to manage all aspects of their one-person businesses effectively.
6. Business Students: Eager to learn practical techniques and frameworks to apply in real-world scenarios.

7. Consultants and Coaches: Seeking resources to help their clients develop and implement effective business strategies.
8. Nonprofit Leaders: Looking for ways to optimize their organizations' operations and achieve their missions more efficiently.
9. Investors: Wanting insights into evaluating business plans and assessing growth potential in various industries.
10. Freelancers: Needing guidance on building sustainable freelance businesses and managing client relationships effectively.
11. Industry Professionals: Seeking to stay ahead of market trends and implement best practices in their respective fields.
12. Managers and Team Leaders: Wanting tools and strategies to enhance team productivity, collaboration, and innovation.
13. Business Coaches and Mentors: Looking for resources to support their clients'

personal and professional development as they navigate business challenges.

14. Creative Entrepreneurs: Needing guidance on balancing artistic vision with sound business principles to achieve creative and financial success.

15. Social Entrepreneurs: Wanting to integrate social impact into their business models and effectively measure their organization's triple bottom line.

16. Retirees Starting Businesses: Seeking guidance on leveraging their experience and skills to launch successful ventures in their post-retirement years.

17. Family-Owned Businesses: Needing strategies to navigate the unique dynamics and challenges of running a business within a family structure.

18. Aspiring Franchisees: Looking for resources to evaluate franchise opportunities, develop business plans, and navigate the franchising process.

19. Career Changers: Wanting guidance on transitioning from traditional employment

to entrepreneurship and building a successful business in a new industry.

20. Global Entrepreneurs: Seeking insights into navigating the complexities of international markets, cross-cultural communication, and global expansion strategies.

I. Introduction

- Welcome and Overview
- Importance of Effective Business Planning

II. Understanding Your Business Landscape

- Market Analysis and Trends
- Competitor Analysis
- SWOT Analysis: Assessing Strengths, Weaknesses, Opportunities, and Threats

III. Crafting Your Business Strategy

- Defining Your Mission, Vision, and Values
- Setting SMART Goals
- Developing Key Strategies and Initiatives

IV. Building a Solid Foundation

- Legal and Regulatory Considerations
- Business Structure Selection
- Financial Planning and Budgeting

V. Marketing and Sales Strategies

- Target Market Identification
- Branding and Positioning
- Marketing Channels and Campaigns
- Sales Funnel Development

VI. Operations and Logistics

- Supply Chain Management
- Inventory Control
- Quality Assurance
- Workflow Optimization

VII. Human Resources and Team Development

- Recruitment and Hiring Processes
- Employee Training and Development
- Performance Management
- Building a Positive Organizational Culture

VIII. Financial Management and Analysis

- Financial Statements Overview
- Cash Flow Management
- Financial Forecasting and Projections
- Cost Control Strategies

IX. Risk Management and Contingency Planning

- Identifying and Assessing Risks
- Developing Risk Mitigation Strategies
- Business Continuity Planning

X. Scaling and Growth Strategies

- Expansion Opportunities Assessment
- Strategic Partnerships and Alliances
- Franchising or Licensing Considerations

XI. Social Responsibility and Sustainability

- Corporate Social Responsibility (CSR)
- Environmental Sustainability Practices
- Social Impact Measurement and Reporting

XII. Technology Integration and Innovation

- Assessing Technology Needs
- Implementing Digital Solutions
- Leveraging Innovation for Competitive Advantage

XIII. Customer Relationship Management

- Building Strong Customer Relationships
- Customer Feedback and Satisfaction Measurement
- Implementing CRM Systems and Strategies

XIV. Adaptation and Agility

- Embracing Change and Adaptation
- Agility in Decision Making
- Pivoting Strategies in Response to Market Shifts

XV. Leadership and Management Skills

- Effective Communication
- Conflict Resolution
- Delegation and Empowerment
- Continuous Learning and Growth

XVI. Exit Strategies and Succession Planning

- Exit Options Evaluation (e.g., IPO, Acquisition, Merger)
- Succession Planning for Leadership Transition
- Ensuring Business Continuity Beyond Founder's Leadership

XVII. Case Studies and Success Stories

- Real-world Examples of Successful Business Planning and Execution
- Lessons Learned from Industry Leaders
- Inspirational Stories of Overcoming Challenges

XVIII. Action Plan and Implementation Guide

- Developing Your Personalized Action Plan

- Step-by-Step Implementation Guide
- Tracking Progress and Adjusting Strategies

XIX. Resources and Tools

- Recommended Books, Articles, and Websites
- Business Planning Templates and Checklists
- Online Courses and Workshops

XX. Conclusion

- Final Thoughts on Achieving Business Success
- Encouragement for Continuous Improvement and Growth
- Thank You and Best Wishes on Your Business Journey

I. Introduction

Welcome to "Charting Success: The Ultimate Business Planner for Thriving Enterprises." In this comprehensive guide, we embark on a journey to unlock the secrets of effective business planning and execution. Whether you're a seasoned entrepreneur, a budding startup founder, or a visionary corporate leader, mastering the art of business planning is essential for achieving sustainable growth and success.

Importance of Effective Business Planning Effective business planning serves as the compass that guides organizations through the ever-evolving landscape of commerce. It provides a roadmap for decision-making, aligns resources with strategic objectives, and empowers teams to navigate challenges with confidence. By carefully charting your course, you can anticipate opportunities, mitigate risks, and steer your enterprise toward its desired destination.

In today's dynamic business environment, the ability to plan strategically is more crucial than ever. Rapid technological advancements, shifting consumer preferences, and global market disruptions demand agility and foresight from businesses of all sizes. Whether you're seeking to launch a new venture, expand into new markets, or enhance operational efficiency, a well-crafted business plan lays the groundwork for success.

Throughout this guide, we'll delve into key principles, proven methodologies, and actionable insights to help you develop a robust business plan tailored to your unique goals and circumstances. From market analysis and financial forecasting to risk management and innovation strategies, each chapter is designed to equip you with the knowledge and tools needed to thrive in today's competitive landscape.

So, join us as we embark on this transformative journey. Together, we'll uncover the strategies, tactics, and best practices that will empower you to chart your path to prosperity and achieve lasting success in the world of business.

Welcome aboard!

II. Understanding Your Business Landscape

In the dynamic realm of business, success hinges on a deep understanding of the landscape in which your enterprise operates. By gaining clarity on market dynamics, competitor positioning, and internal capabilities, you can formulate strategies that capitalize on opportunities and mitigate risks effectively. In this section, we explore the essential components of understanding your business landscape, including market analysis, competitor analysis, and SWOT analysis.

Market Analysis and Trends

A thorough market analysis is the cornerstone of effective business planning. It involves assessing market size, growth potential, customer demographics, and emerging trends that could impact your industry. By studying market dynamics, you can identify unmet needs, emerging opportunities, and potential areas for differentiation. Whether you're entering a new market or seeking to consolidate your position in an existing one, a comprehensive understanding of market trends is essential for informed decision-making and strategic planning.

Competitor Analysis

In today's fiercely competitive business landscape, knowing your competitors is paramount. Competitor analysis involves evaluating the strengths and weaknesses of rival firms and understanding their market positioning, product offerings, pricing strategies, and customer segments. By benchmarking your performance against competitors, you can identify areas of competitive advantage and areas for improvement. Additionally, studying competitor behavior can reveal valuable insights into market dynamics, customer preferences, and emerging threats.

SWOT Analysis: Assessing Strengths, Weaknesses, Opportunities, and Threats

A SWOT analysis is a powerful tool for assessing your organization's internal strengths and weaknesses, as well as external opportunities and threats. By conducting a systematic examination of these factors, you can develop strategies that leverage your strengths, address your weaknesses, capitalize on opportunities, and mitigate threats. Whether you're evaluating a new business venture, launching a new product, or formulating a growth strategy, a SWOT analysis provides valuable insights that inform decision-making and guide strategic direction.

In the subsequent chapters, we will delve deeper into each of these components, providing practical frameworks, tools, and techniques to conduct comprehensive analyses and extract actionable insights. By mastering the art of understanding your business landscape, you'll be better equipped to navigate challenges, capitalize on opportunities, and chart a course toward sustainable growth and success.

III. Crafting Your Business Strategy:

Crafting a robust business strategy is essential for the long-term success and sustainability of any organization. This section delves into the fundamental steps involved in shaping a comprehensive business strategy:

Defining Your Mission, Vision, and Values

1. Mission Statement: This succinctly articulates the purpose and reason for the existence of the business. It outlines what the organization does, who it serves, and why it matters.
2. Vision Statement: A forward-looking declaration of the desired future state of the organization. It encapsulates the aspirations and long-term goals that the company aims to achieve.
3. Values: These represent the guiding principles and beliefs that shape the culture and behavior of the organization. They serve as the moral compass, influencing decision-making and actions at all levels.

Setting SMART Goals

1. Specific: Goals should be clear, well-defined, and focused, leaving no room for ambiguity or misunderstanding.
2. Measurable: Goals should be quantifiable, allowing progress to be tracked and measured objectively.
3. Achievable: Goals should be realistic and attainable within the resources, capabilities, and constraints of the organization.
4. Relevant: Goals should align with the overall mission, vision, and strategic priorities of the business, contributing meaningfully to its success.
5. Time-bound: Goals should have a defined timeframe or deadline, providing a sense of urgency and accountability.

Developing Key Strategies and Initiatives

1. Strategic Priorities: Identify the key areas or themes that will drive the organization's success and competitive advantage. These priorities should align with the mission,

vision, and values while addressing critical challenges and opportunities.

2. Strategic Initiatives: Concrete actions and projects designed to execute the strategic priorities and achieve the defined goals. These initiatives should be well-planned, resourced, and executed with precision to deliver desired outcomes.

3. Resource Allocation: Allocate resources such as capital, talent, and time effectively to support the execution of strategic initiatives. Ensure alignment with strategic priorities and continuous evaluation to optimize resource utilization.

4. Risk Management: Identify and assess potential risks and uncertainties that may impact the achievement of strategic objectives. Develop mitigation strategies and contingency plans to minimize disruptions and capitalize on emerging opportunities.

Crafting a business strategy requires careful consideration, collaboration, and ongoing refinement. By defining a clear mission, vision, and values, setting SMART goals, and developing key strategies and initiatives, organizations can navigate complexities, capitalize on opportunities, and achieve sustainable growth in an ever-evolving business landscape.

IV. Building a Solid Foundation:

Establishing a solid foundation is imperative for the success and longevity of any business venture. This section explores the critical aspects involved in laying a robust groundwork for your enterprise:

Legal and Regulatory Considerations

1. Compliance: Familiarize yourself with the relevant laws, regulations, and industry standards that govern your business operations. Ensure full compliance with requirements related to permits, licenses, taxation, employment laws, data protection, and other legal obligations.

2. Intellectual Property Protection: Safeguard your intellectual property assets, including trademarks, patents, copyrights, and trade secrets. Implement measures to prevent infringement and unauthorized use, and consider seeking legal advice to secure and enforce your intellectual property rights.

3. Contracts and Agreements: Draft, review, and negotiate contracts and agreements with suppliers, partners, customers, and other stakeholders. Clearly define rights, responsibilities, terms, and conditions to mitigate risks and establish mutually beneficial relationships.

Business Structure Selection

1. Legal Entity: Choose the most appropriate legal structure for your business, considering factors such as liability protection, taxation, management flexibility, and regulatory requirements. Options may include sole proprietorship, partnership, limited liability company (LLC), corporation, or cooperative.
2. Corporate Governance: Establish sound corporate governance practices to ensure transparency, accountability, and ethical conduct within your organization. Define roles and responsibilities, establish decision-making processes, and

implement internal controls to promote integrity and mitigate risks.

Financial Planning and Budgeting

1. Financial Forecasting: Develop realistic financial projections and forecasts based on thorough market research, historical data, and industry trends. Estimate revenues, expenses, cash flow, and profitability to inform strategic decision-making and resource allocation.

2. Budgeting: Create a comprehensive budget that aligns with your strategic goals and operational plans. Allocate resources effectively across various departments and initiatives, taking into account short-term priorities and long-term objectives.

3. Capital Management: Identify sources of capital to fund your business activities, including equity financing, debt financing, grants, and bootstrapping. Evaluate the costs, risks, and terms associated with each option and develop a capital strategy

that balances growth objectives with financial sustainability.

4. Financial Controls: Implement robust financial controls and monitoring mechanisms to track performance, detect deviations from planned outcomes, and address variances promptly. Regularly review financial reports, key performance indicators (KPIs), and metrics to assess progress and make informed adjustments as needed.

Building a solid foundation involves navigating complex legal and regulatory landscapes, selecting the right business structure, and implementing sound financial planning and budgeting practices. By addressing these critical considerations effectively, entrepreneurs can establish a strong footing for their ventures and enhance their prospects for long-term success and viability.

V. Marketing and Sales Strategies:

Developing effective marketing and sales strategies is essential for reaching and engaging with target customers, driving brand awareness, and ultimately generating revenue. This section explores key elements of crafting successful marketing and sales strategies:

Target Market Identification

1. Market Segmentation: Divide the broader market into distinct segments based on characteristics such as demographics, psychographics, behavior, and needs. This enables more targeted and personalized marketing efforts tailored to specific customer groups.

2. Customer Profiling: Develop detailed profiles of ideal customers within each segment, including their preferences, pain points, purchasing behavior, and communication preferences. Use market research, surveys, and data analytics to gain insights into customer motivations and preferences.

Branding and Positioning

1. Brand Identity: Define your brand identity, including your brand purpose, values, personality, and visual elements such as logo, colors, typography, and imagery. Ensure consistency in brand messaging and visual identity across all touchpoints to build brand recognition and trust.

2. Positioning Strategy: Determine how you want your brand to be perceived relative to competitors in the minds of consumers. Identify unique selling propositions (USPs) and positioning statements that differentiate your brand and resonate with your target audience.

Marketing Channels and Campaigns

1. Multi-channel Approach: Select the most appropriate marketing channels to reach your target audience effectively. This may include digital channels such as social media, search engine marketing, email marketing, and content marketing, as well

as traditional channels like print, television, radio, and events.

2. Integrated Campaigns: Develop integrated marketing campaigns that leverage multiple channels and tactics to create a cohesive and consistent brand experience. Align messaging, creative assets, and promotional offers across different touchpoints to maximize reach and impact.

Sales Funnel Development

1. Awareness Stage: Attract potential customers and generate awareness through content marketing, social media engagement, search engine optimization (SEO), and advertising.
2. Interest and Consideration Stage: Nurture leads and engage prospects by providing valuable content, personalized communications, product demonstrations, and educational resources.
3. Decision Stage: Convert leads into customers by highlighting product

features, benefits, testimonials, and special offers. Use persuasive sales tactics, retargeting campaigns, and personalized incentives to encourage purchase decisions.

4. Retention and Advocacy Stage: Delight customers post-purchase by providing exceptional service, support, and incentives for loyalty and advocacy. Encourage satisfied customers to share their experiences, refer others, and become brand ambassadors.

By identifying target markets, establishing a strong brand presence, leveraging diverse marketing channels, and implementing a well-defined sales funnel, businesses can effectively engage with customers, drive sales, and foster long-term relationships. Continuous monitoring, analysis, and optimization of marketing and sales strategies are essential to adapt to changing market dynamics and maximize performance.

VI. Operations and Logistics

Efficient operations and logistics management are crucial for delivering products and services effectively, optimizing resources, and meeting customer demands. This section explores key aspects of operations and logistics:

Supply Chain Management

1. Supplier Selection and Management: Identify reliable suppliers who can consistently provide high-quality materials or components at competitive prices. Establish strong relationships and communication channels to ensure timely delivery and address any issues promptly.

2. Inventory Management: Optimize inventory levels to balance the cost of holding inventory with the risk of stockouts. Implement inventory control techniques such as just-in-time (JIT) inventory, economic order quantity (EOQ), and ABC analysis to minimize carrying costs while maintaining adequate stock levels.

Inventory Control

1. Demand Forecasting: Use historical sales data, market trends, and customer insights to forecast demand accurately. Adjust inventory levels based on demand forecasts to prevent excess inventory or stockouts.

2. Inventory Tracking and Monitoring: Implement inventory tracking systems and processes to monitor stock levels, movements, and turnover in real time. Utilize barcoding, RFID, or inventory management software to streamline inventory control and improve accuracy.

Quality Assurance

1. Quality Standards and Procedures: Establish clear quality standards, specifications, and procedures for all products and processes. Ensure compliance with industry regulations, standards, and certifications to meet customer expectations and regulatory requirements.

2. Quality Control Inspections: Conduct regular inspections and quality checks at various stages of production to identify and rectify defects or deviations from quality standards. Implement quality control tools and techniques such as statistical process control (SPC) and Six Sigma to continuously improve quality.

Workflow Optimization

1. Process Analysis and Improvement: Analyze existing workflows and processes to identify inefficiencies, bottlenecks, and areas for improvement. Streamline processes, eliminate waste, and optimize resource allocation to enhance productivity and reduce costs.

2. Automation and Technology Integration: Leverage automation tools, technology solutions, and software systems to automate repetitive tasks, streamline workflows, and improve efficiency. Implement enterprise resource planning (ERP), warehouse management systems

(WMS), and transportation management systems (TMS) to integrate and synchronize operations.

3. Continuous Improvement Culture: Foster a culture of continuous improvement and innovation within the organization. Encourage employees to identify and implement process improvements, share best practices, and participate in training and development programs to enhance skills and knowledge.

Effective operations and logistics management involves optimizing supply chains, controlling inventory, ensuring quality, and optimizing workflows. By implementing best practices, leveraging technology, and fostering a culture of continuous improvement, businesses can enhance efficiency, reduce costs, and deliver value to customers consistently.

VII. Human Resources and Team Development:

A strong human resources (HR) function is essential for attracting, retaining, and developing talent, as well as fostering a positive organizational culture. This section explores key elements of HR and team development:

Recruitment and Hiring Processes

1. Talent Acquisition Strategy: Develop a comprehensive recruitment strategy aligned with the organization's goals and workforce needs. Identify sourcing channels, including job boards, social media, referrals, and recruitment agencies, to attract top talent.

2. Candidate Selection and Assessment: Implement structured selection processes, including resume screening, interviews, and assessments, to evaluate candidates based on skills, experience, cultural fit, and potential. Ensure fairness, transparency, and compliance with equal

employment opportunity (EEO) laws and regulations.

Employee Training and Development

1. Training Needs Analysis: Assess the skills, knowledge, and competencies required for each role and identify training gaps and development opportunities. Develop tailored training programs to address specific needs and support employee growth and career advancement.
2. Continuous Learning Culture: Foster a culture of continuous learning and development by providing access to training resources, workshops, seminars, and online learning platforms. Encourage employees to take ownership of their professional development and pursue growth opportunities.

Performance Management

1. Goal Setting and Alignment: Set clear and measurable performance goals that align

with the organization's objectives and individual roles. Establish key performance indicators (KPIs) to track progress and evaluate performance effectively.

2. Regular Feedback and Coaching: Provide ongoing feedback and coaching to employees to support their development, address performance issues, and recognize achievements. Conduct regular performance reviews and check-ins to assess progress, discuss goals, and provide guidance.

Building a Positive Organizational Culture

1. Values and Behaviors: Define core values and desired behaviors that reflect the organization's identity and promote a positive work environment. Lead by example and reinforce values through communication, recognition, and rewards.

2. Employee Engagement Initiatives: Implement initiatives to foster employee engagement, collaboration, and morale.

This may include team-building activities, social events, wellness programs, and opportunities for community involvement.

3. Inclusion and Diversity: Promote inclusion and diversity within the workplace by embracing differences and creating a culture of respect, acceptance, and belonging. Ensure equal opportunities for all employees and create a supportive environment where everyone can thrive.

4. Work-Life Balance: Encourage work-life balance by offering flexible work arrangements, remote work options, and benefits such as paid time off, parental leave, and wellness benefits. Support employees in managing their responsibilities both inside and outside of work.

By focusing on recruitment and hiring processes, employee training and development, performance management, and building a positive organizational culture, HR professionals can effectively support the growth and success of their teams and contribute to the overall success of the organization.

VIII. Financial Management and Analysis:

Sound financial management and analysis are essential for ensuring the financial health and sustainability of an organization. This section delves into key aspects of financial management and analysis:

Financial Statements Overview

1. Balance Sheet: Provides a snapshot of the organization's financial position at a specific point in time, detailing assets, liabilities, and equity. It showcases the company's liquidity, solvency, and overall financial health.
2. Income Statement: Summarizes the organization's revenues, expenses, and profitability over a specific period, typically monthly, quarterly, or annually. It helps stakeholders assess the company's ability to generate profits and manage expenses effectively.

3. Cash Flow Statement: Tracks the inflow and outflow of cash and cash equivalents during a specific period, categorizing cash flows into operating, investing, and financing activities. It provides insights into the organization's liquidity and cash management practices.

Cash Flow Management

1. Cash Flow Forecasting: Project future cash inflows and outflows to anticipate potential cash shortages or surpluses. Develop cash flow projections based on historical data, sales forecasts, and expense estimates to inform decision-making and mitigate liquidity risks.
2. Working Capital Management: Manage working capital efficiently to ensure adequate liquidity for day-to-day operations while optimizing the use of resources. Monitor accounts receivable, accounts payable, and inventory levels to minimize cash tied up in working capital.

Financial Forecasting and Projections

1. Revenue Forecasting: Estimate future revenues based on market trends, sales forecasts, and historical performance. Consider factors such as seasonality, market demand, and competitive dynamics to develop realistic revenue projections.
2. Expense Projections: Anticipate future expenses across various categories, including operating expenses, capital expenditures, and overhead costs. Analyze historical spending patterns and market trends to forecast expenses accurately.

Cost Control Strategies

1. Cost Analysis: Conduct a thorough cost analysis to identify cost drivers, inefficiencies, and areas for cost reduction or optimization. Analyze direct costs, indirect costs, and overhead expenses to identify opportunities for cost savings.
2. Budgeting and Variance Analysis: Develop detailed budgets that align with

strategic objectives and financial targets. Monitor actual performance against budgeted figures and conduct variance analysis to identify deviations and take corrective actions.

3. Efficiency Improvements: Implement efficiency improvement initiatives to streamline processes, eliminate waste, and reduce operating costs. Embrace lean principles, automation, and technology solutions to enhance productivity and resource utilization.

4. Negotiation and Supplier Management: Negotiate favorable terms with suppliers and vendors to secure competitive pricing, discounts, and payment terms. Establish strategic partnerships and leverage economies of scale to achieve cost savings.

By leveraging financial statements for insights, implementing effective cash flow management practices, conducting accurate financial forecasting and projections, and implementing cost control strategies, organizations can enhance their financial performance, mitigate risks, and achieve sustainable growth in a dynamic business environment.

IX. Risk Management and Contingency Planning:

Effective risk management and contingency planning are essential for safeguarding business operations, protecting assets, and ensuring resilience in the face of uncertainties. This section explores key components of risk management and contingency planning:

Identifying and Assessing Risks

1. Risk Identification: Conduct a comprehensive assessment to identify potential risks and vulnerabilities that may impact the organization's objectives, operations, or stakeholders. Consider internal and external factors, such as market risks, regulatory changes, operational disruptions, and cybersecurity threats.

2. Risk Analysis: Evaluate the likelihood and potential impact of identified risks on the organization using qualitative and quantitative methods. Prioritize risks

based on their severity, frequency, and significance to the business.

Developing Risk Mitigation Strategies

1. Risk Avoidance: Take proactive measures to eliminate or avoid high-risk activities, situations, or exposures that pose significant threats to the organization. This may involve revising processes, discontinuing products or services, or exiting high-risk markets.

2. Risk Reduction: Implement controls, safeguards, and risk mitigation measures to reduce the likelihood or severity of identified risks. Enhance security measures, implement redundancy, and improve internal controls to mitigate operational, financial, and reputational risks.

3. Risk Transfer: Transfer risk to third parties through insurance, contracts, or other risk-sharing mechanisms. Purchase appropriate insurance coverage to protect against losses from events such as

property damage, liability claims, or business interruptions.

Business Continuity Planning

1. Business Impact Analysis: Assess the potential impact of disruptive events on critical business functions, processes, and resources. Identify dependencies, recovery time objectives (RTOs), and recovery point objectives (RPOs) to prioritize continuity efforts.

2. Developing Continuity Plans: Develop detailed business continuity plans outlining procedures, protocols, and responsibilities for responding to and recovering from various scenarios. Define roles and responsibilities, establish communication protocols, and document recovery procedures.

3. Testing and Training: Conduct regular testing and drills to validate the effectiveness of business continuity plans and ensure readiness to respond to emergencies. Provide training and

awareness programs to educate employees on their roles and responsibilities during a crisis.

4. Continuous Improvement: Review and update business continuity plans regularly to reflect changes in the business environment, technology, or regulatory requirements. Incorporate lessons learned from past incidents and exercises to enhance preparedness and resilience.

By systematically identifying and assessing risks, developing robust mitigation strategies, and implementing comprehensive business continuity plans, organizations can enhance their ability to anticipate, respond to, and recover from disruptive events. Effective risk management and contingency planning are essential components of a proactive approach to managing uncertainties and protecting business interests.

X. Scaling and Growth Strategies:

Scaling and growth are pivotal phases in the evolution of any business, requiring careful assessment of expansion opportunities and strategic planning. This section delves into key strategies for scaling and achieving sustainable growth:

Expansion Opportunities Assessment

1. Market Analysis: Conduct thorough market research to identify growth opportunities, emerging trends, and customer needs. Assess market dynamics, competitive landscape, and demand patterns to inform expansion strategies.

2. Product or Service Diversification: Explore opportunities to diversify your product or service offerings to appeal to new customer segments or address unmet needs in existing markets. Consider expanding into related industries or complementary product lines to leverage existing capabilities and resources.

1. Strategic Collaborations: Form partnerships and alliances with complementary businesses, suppliers, distributors, or technology providers to enhance capabilities, expand reach, and access new markets. Collaborate on joint ventures, co-marketing campaigns, or product development initiatives to create synergies and mutual benefits.

2. Acquisitions and Mergers: Evaluate opportunities for mergers or acquisitions to accelerate growth, acquire new capabilities, or gain access to new markets. Assess potential targets based on strategic fit, financial viability, and integration potential to maximize value creation.

Franchising or Licensing Considerations

1. Franchise Model: Explore franchising as a scalable growth strategy to expand your brand presence and distribution network. Develop a franchise model that provides

franchisees with a proven business concept, comprehensive training, and ongoing support to ensure consistency and quality standards.

2. Licensing Agreements: Consider licensing your intellectual property, trademarks, or proprietary technology to third parties in exchange for royalties or licensing fees. Evaluate potential licensees based on their reputation, capabilities, and alignment with your brand values.

Sustainable Growth Strategies

1. Operational Efficiency: Streamline processes, optimize resource allocation, and leverage technology to improve operational efficiency and scalability. Invest in automation, systems integration, and lean practices to reduce costs and enhance productivity.

2. Customer Retention and Loyalty: Focus on building long-term relationships with existing customers through exceptional service, personalized experiences, and

loyalty programs. Retaining customers is often more cost-effective than acquiring new ones and can drive sustainable revenue growth.

3. Talent Acquisition and Development: Invest in recruiting and retaining top talent to fuel growth and innovation. Develop a culture of learning and development to empower employees to contribute to the organization's success and adapt to evolving business needs.

4. Financial Planning and Capital Allocation: Develop a robust financial plan that supports growth initiatives while maintaining financial stability and sustainability. Allocate capital strategically to fund expansion projects, manage cash flow effectively, and mitigate financial risks.

Scaling and achieving sustainable growth requires a strategic approach that balances expansion opportunities with operational considerations, partnerships, and financial planning. By assessing expansion opportunities, forging strategic partnerships, and implementing scalable growth strategies, businesses can position themselves for long-term success and competitiveness in dynamic markets.

XI. Social Responsibility and Sustainability:

In today's business landscape, corporate social responsibility (CSR) and sustainability are integral components of a company's identity and success. This section explores key aspects of social responsibility and sustainability:

Corporate Social Responsibility (CSR)

1. Stakeholder Engagement: Engage with stakeholders including customers, employees, communities, suppliers, and investors to understand their expectations and concerns regarding social and environmental issues. Incorporate stakeholder feedback into CSR initiatives to enhance transparency and accountability.

2. Community Engagement and Philanthropy: Develop community outreach programs, charitable initiatives, and volunteer opportunities to support local communities and address social

needs. Partner with nonprofit organizations, NGOs, and community groups to maximize impact and leverage resources effectively.

Environmental Sustainability Practices

1. Resource Conservation: Implement measures to reduce resource consumption, minimize waste generation, and conserve energy and water resources. Adopt sustainable practices such as recycling, energy efficiency improvements, and water conservation measures to minimize environmental impact.
2. Climate Action: Take proactive steps to mitigate climate change impacts and reduce greenhouse gas emissions. Set targets for carbon footprint reduction, invest in renewable energy sources, and implement sustainable transportation and logistics practices to contribute to climate resilience and sustainability.

Social Impact Measurement and Reporting

1. Impact Assessment: Evaluate the social and environmental impact of CSR initiatives using measurable metrics and indicators. Monitor progress against predefined goals and targets, and assess the effectiveness and outcomes of social programs and sustainability initiatives.

2. Transparency and Reporting: Communicate CSR activities, environmental performance, and social impact through transparent reporting and disclosure mechanisms. Publish annual sustainability reports, participate in sustainability indices, and engage with stakeholders through regular communication channels to build trust and credibility.

Ethical Business Practices

1. Fair Labor Practices: Ensure compliance with labor laws, uphold labor rights, and promote fair and equitable treatment of employees throughout the supply chain.

Provide safe working conditions, fair wages, and opportunities for professional development and advancement.

2. Ethical Sourcing and Supply Chain Management: Implement ethical sourcing practices and supply chain due diligence to prevent human rights abuses, child labor, and environmental degradation. Collaborate with suppliers to promote responsible sourcing, ethical production practices, and supply chain transparency.

Incorporating CSR and sustainability into business operations fosters long-term value creation, enhances brand reputation, and strengthens stakeholder relationships. By embracing social responsibility, environmental stewardship, and ethical business practices, organizations can contribute to positive social and environmental outcomes while driving business success and sustainable growth.

XII. Technology Integration and Innovation:

Technology integration and innovation play a pivotal role in driving business growth, enhancing operational efficiency, and maintaining competitiveness in today's digital age. This section explores key aspects of technology integration and innovation:

Assessing Technology Needs

1. Business Objectives Alignment: Align technology initiatives with business objectives and strategic priorities. Identify areas where technology can drive value creation, improve processes, or address operational challenges effectively.

2. Gap Analysis: Conduct a thorough assessment of current systems, processes, and capabilities to identify gaps and inefficiencies that technology solutions can address. Evaluate existing technology infrastructure, software applications, and

IT resources to determine areas for improvement.

Implementing Digital Solutions

1. Digital Transformation Strategy: Develop a comprehensive digital transformation strategy that outlines the vision, goals, and roadmap for leveraging technology to transform business operations and customer experiences. Prioritize initiatives based on their impact and feasibility.

2. Technology Adoption: Implement digital solutions that align with business needs and provide tangible benefits such as increased efficiency, productivity, and customer satisfaction. Deploy cloud computing, data analytics, artificial intelligence (AI), and Internet of Things (IoT) technologies to optimize operations and enable innovation.

Leveraging Innovation for Competitive Advantage

1. Culture of Innovation: Foster a culture of innovation that encourages creativity, experimentation, and continuous improvement across the organization. Empower employees to propose new ideas, explore emerging technologies, and embrace change as opportunities for growth.

2. Collaboration and Partnerships: Collaborate with technology partners, startups, academic institutions, and industry experts to access cutting-edge technologies, expertise, and resources. Form strategic partnerships to co-develop innovative solutions, pilot new technologies, or enter new markets.

3. Agile Development: Embrace agile methodologies and iterative development approaches to accelerate innovation and adapt to changing market demands. Prioritize innovation projects based on strategic alignment, customer feedback,

and market trends to maximize impact and value creation.

4. Customer-Centric Innovation: Listen to customer feedback, anticipate their evolving needs, and innovate proactively to deliver superior products, services, and experiences. Leverage customer data, user research, and design thinking principles to inform innovation efforts and drive customer satisfaction and loyalty.

By assessing technology needs, implementing digital solutions, and leveraging innovation for competitive advantage, organizations can stay ahead of the curve, drive business growth, and deliver value to customers in an increasingly digital and dynamic marketplace. Embracing technology integration and innovation as strategic imperatives enables organizations to unlock new opportunities, overcome challenges, and thrive in the digital economy.

XIII. Customer Relationship Management:

Customer relationship management (CRM) is a critical component of business success, focusing on building strong relationships with customers, understanding their needs, and delivering exceptional experiences. This section explores key aspects of CRM:

Building Strong Customer Relationships

1. Personalized Interactions: Engage with customers on a personal level by understanding their preferences, behaviors, and unique needs. Tailor interactions and communications to provide personalized experiences that demonstrate care and empathy.
2. Effective Communication: Foster open and transparent communication channels to establish trust and rapport with customers. Proactively reach out to customers to provide updates, address

concerns, and solicit feedback to ensure their needs are met.

3. Consistent Service Excellence: Deliver consistent and high-quality service across all touchpoints, whether it's in-person interactions, online support, or social media engagement. Strive to exceed customer expectations and create memorable experiences that drive loyalty and advocacy.

Customer Feedback and Satisfaction Measurement

1. Feedback Collection: Implement systems and processes to gather feedback from customers at various touchpoints throughout their journey. Use surveys, feedback forms, reviews, and social media monitoring to capture insights into customer satisfaction, preferences, and pain points.

2. Data Analysis: Analyze customer feedback and satisfaction metrics to identify trends, patterns, and areas for

improvement. Use data-driven insights to prioritize initiatives, address systemic issues, and enhance the overall customer experience.

Implementing CRM Systems and Strategies

1. CRM System Selection: Choose a CRM platform that aligns with your business needs, goals, and budget. Evaluate features such as contact management, sales automation, marketing automation, and customer service capabilities to support your CRM strategy.
2. Integration with Business Processes: Integrate CRM systems seamlessly into existing business processes and workflows to maximize efficiency and effectiveness. Ensure alignment with sales, marketing, and customer service functions to enable cross-functional collaboration and data sharing.
3. Training and Adoption: Provide comprehensive training and support to employees to ensure proper use and

adoption of CRM systems and strategies. Empower teams with the skills and knowledge needed to leverage CRM tools effectively in their daily operations.

4. Continuous Improvement: Regularly review and refine CRM strategies based on performance metrics, customer feedback, and changing market dynamics. Continuously optimize processes, workflows, and technology solutions to adapt to evolving customer needs and preferences.

Benefits of Effective CRM

1. Customer Retention: By nurturing strong relationships and delivering exceptional experiences, effective CRM practices can enhance customer loyalty and retention rates.

2. Increased Sales and Revenue: A well-implemented CRM strategy can drive sales growth by enabling more targeted marketing campaigns, better lead

management, and improved sales pipeline management.

3. Improved Efficiency: Streamlined processes and automation features in CRM systems can increase operational efficiency, reduce manual tasks, and empower employees to focus on high-value activities.

4. Enhanced Customer Insights: By centralizing customer data and feedback, CRM systems provide valuable insights into customer behavior, preferences, and trends, enabling data-driven decision-making and personalized marketing efforts.

By prioritizing customer relationships, collecting and acting on feedback, and implementing effective CRM systems and strategies, organizations can build lasting connections with customers, drive business growth, and maintain a competitive edge in today's dynamic marketplace.

XIV. Adaptation and Agility:

In today's rapidly changing business environment, organizations must embrace adaptation and agility to thrive amidst uncertainty and complexity. This section explores key aspects of adaptation and agility:

Embracing Change and Adaptation

1. Change Management: Cultivate a culture that embraces change as an opportunity for growth and innovation rather than a threat. Encourage employees to adopt a growth mindset and remain flexible and adaptable in the face of evolving market dynamics.

2. Continuous Learning: Foster a learning organization where employees are encouraged to seek new knowledge, acquire new skills, and adapt to changing circumstances. Invest in training and development programs to build resilience and agility at all levels of the organization.

Agility in Decision Making

1. Real-Time Data Analysis: Leverage data analytics and business intelligence tools to gather real-time insights into market trends, customer preferences, and competitive dynamics. Use data-driven decision-making to respond swiftly to changing conditions and opportunities.
2. Decentralized Decision-Making: Empower frontline employees and cross-functional teams to make decisions autonomously within defined parameters. Distribute decision-making authority to those closest to the action to enable faster responses and greater agility.

Pivoting Strategies in Response to Market Shifts

1. Scenario Planning: Anticipate potential market shifts, disruptions, and uncertainties by conducting scenario planning exercises. Develop contingency plans and alternative strategies to adapt quickly to different scenarios and mitigate risks effectively.

2. Iterative Approach: Embrace an iterative approach to strategy development and execution, allowing for experimentation, learning, and adaptation over time. Monitor market feedback, customer reactions, and performance metrics to iterate and refine strategies as needed.

3. Agile Methodologies: Adopt agile methodologies such as Scrum or Kanban to manage projects and initiatives with flexibility and adaptability. Break down projects into smaller, manageable tasks, prioritize based on value, and iterate quickly based on feedback and changing priorities.

Benefits of Adaptation and Agility

1. Competitive Advantage: Organizations that are agile and adaptive can respond more effectively to market shifts, emerging trends, and competitive threats, gaining a competitive edge in the marketplace.

2. Innovation and Growth: Adaptation and agility foster a culture of innovation and experimentation, driving continuous improvement and enabling organizations to seize new growth opportunities.
3. Resilience: Agile organizations are better equipped to navigate disruptions, crises, and unexpected challenges, maintaining stability and continuity in the face of adversity.
4. Customer Satisfaction: By responding quickly to customer needs and preferences, agile organizations can deliver superior customer experiences and build stronger relationships with their target audience.

By embracing change and adaptation, practicing agility in decision-making, and pivoting strategies in response to market shifts, organizations can navigate uncertainty with confidence, seize growth opportunities, and sustain success in an ever-evolving business landscape.

XV. Leadership and Management Skills:

Effective leadership and management skills are essential for guiding teams, driving performance, and fostering a culture of success within organizations. This section explores key skills and practices for effective leadership and management:

Effective Communication

1. Clear and Transparent Communication: Communicate vision, goals, and expectations clearly and transparently to ensure alignment and understanding among team members. Use active listening, empathy, and feedback mechanisms to promote open communication and address concerns effectively.

2. Adaptability in Communication Style: Tailor communication style and delivery to suit the needs and preferences of different individuals and situations. Adjust

tone, language, and messaging to ensure messages resonate and are understood by diverse audiences.

Conflict Resolution

1. Active Conflict Management: Proactively address conflicts and disagreements that arise within teams or between individuals. Encourage open dialogue, perspective-taking, and collaborative problem-solving to resolve conflicts constructively and prevent escalation.
2. Mediation and Negotiation Skills: Develop mediation and negotiation skills to facilitate discussions, find common ground, and reach mutually beneficial resolutions. Remain impartial, fair, and empathetic when mediating conflicts to maintain trust and credibility.

Delegation and Empowerment

1. Effective Delegation: Delegate tasks and responsibilities to team members based on their skills, expertise, and development

goals. Provide clear instructions, resources, and support to empower individuals to take ownership and accountability for their work.

2. Empowerment and Autonomy: Foster a culture of empowerment by trusting employees to make decisions, take initiative, and solve problems independently. Provide autonomy and autonomy and encourage experimentation and innovation to unleash potential and drive performance.

Continuous Learning and Growth

1. Commitment to Lifelong Learning: Lead by example and demonstrate a commitment to continuous learning and personal growth. Encourage team members to pursue professional development opportunities, acquire new skills, and stay abreast of industry trends and best practices.

2. Feedback and Performance Coaching: Provide regular feedback, coaching, and

mentorship to support individual growth and development. Identify strengths, areas for improvement, and opportunities for skill enhancement to help team members reach their full potential.

Benefits of Effective Leadership and Management Skills

1. High-Performing Teams: Effective leadership and management skills enable teams to collaborate effectively, stay motivated, and achieve high levels of performance and productivity.
2. Employee Engagement and Satisfaction: Strong leadership fosters a positive work environment where employees feel valued, empowered, and motivated to contribute their best efforts.
3. Conflict Resolution and Collaboration: By mastering conflict resolution techniques and promoting open communication, leaders can foster collaboration, trust, and teamwork within their teams and across the organization.

4. Organizational Resilience and Adaptability: Effective leaders guide organizations through change and uncertainty with resilience and adaptability, inspiring confidence and stability amidst challenges.

By honing effective communication, conflict resolution, delegation, and continuous learning skills, leaders and managers can inspire and empower their teams to achieve excellence, drive innovation, and foster a culture of continuous improvement and growth within the organization.

XVI. Exit Strategies and Succession Planning:

Planning for the eventual exit of a business owner or leader is a crucial aspect of long-term sustainability and continuity. This section explores key considerations for exit strategies and succession planning:

Exit Options Evaluation

1. IPO (Initial Public Offering): Consider going public as an option for raising capital and unlocking shareholder value. Evaluate the requirements, costs, and potential benefits of an IPO, including increased liquidity, access to public markets, and brand visibility.

2. Acquisition: Explore the possibility of selling the business to a strategic buyer or investor. Assess potential acquirers, their strategic fit, valuation expectations, and cultural alignment to ensure a successful transaction that maximizes value for stakeholders.

3. Merger: Explore merger opportunities with complementary businesses or competitors to achieve synergies, economies of scale, and market expansion. Evaluate potential merger partners based on strategic alignment, operational fit, and growth potential.

Succession Planning for Leadership Transition

1. Identifying Successors: Identify potential successors within the organization who have the skills, experience, and leadership qualities to assume key leadership roles. Develop a talent pipeline and succession plan to groom and prepare future leaders for their roles.

2. Leadership Development: Invest in leadership development programs, mentoring, and coaching to develop and nurture the next generation of leaders. Provide opportunities for high-potential employees to gain exposure to different areas of the business and develop leadership competencies.

Ensuring Business Continuity Beyond Founder's Leadership

1. Documenting Processes and Procedures: Document critical business processes, systems, and procedures to ensure continuity and minimize disruption during leadership transitions. Create a knowledge repository and succession playbook to guide future leaders and ensure smooth operations.

2. Building Organizational Resilience: Foster a culture of resilience and adaptability within the organization to navigate leadership changes and external disruptions effectively. Develop contingency plans and risk mitigation strategies to address potential challenges and uncertainties.

3. Stakeholder Communication: Communicate transparently with stakeholders, including employees, customers, suppliers, and investors, about leadership transitions and succession plans. Provide reassurance and clarity

about the organization's direction and commitment to continuity and stability.

Benefits of Effective Exit Strategies and Succession Planning

1. Smooth Transitions: Effective exit strategies and succession planning ensure smooth leadership transitions and minimize disruption to business operations and stakeholders.
2. Business Continuity: By preparing for leadership changes and contingencies, organizations can maintain continuity and stability, even in the absence of the founder or key leaders.
3. Maximized Value: Thoughtful evaluation of exit options and succession planning strategies can maximize value for stakeholders, whether through an IPO, acquisition, or merger.
4. Long-Term Sustainability: Exit strategies and succession planning contribute to the long-term sustainability and resilience of the organization, ensuring its continued

success beyond the tenure of its founders
or current leaders.

By evaluating exit options, implementing succession plans, and ensuring business continuity, organizations can navigate leadership transitions successfully and position themselves for sustained growth and success in the long term.

XVII. Case Studies and Success Stories:

Examining real-world examples of successful business planning, execution, and overcoming challenges provides valuable insights and inspiration for organizations seeking to learn from industry leaders. This section presents case studies and success stories:

Real-World Examples of Successful Business Planning and Execution

1. Amazon: Amazon's relentless focus on customer obsession, innovation, and long-term thinking has propelled it to become one of the world's largest and most successful companies. Through strategic acquisitions, investments in technology, and a commitment to operational excellence, Amazon has transformed multiple industries and redefined customer expectations.

2. Tesla: Tesla's disruptive approach to the automotive industry has revolutionized the

perception of electric vehicles and sustainable transportation. By combining cutting-edge technology, visionary leadership, and a bold mission to accelerate the world's transition to sustainable energy, Tesla has achieved remarkable growth and market dominance.

Lessons Learned from Industry Leaders

1. Apple: Apple's commitment to product innovation, design excellence, and ecosystem integration has set it apart as a leader in the technology industry. Key lessons from Apple include the importance of customer-centric design, brand loyalty, and a relentless focus on quality and user experience.
2. Google: Google's success can be attributed to its culture of innovation, data-driven decision-making, and relentless pursuit of moonshot projects. Lessons from Google include the value of experimentation, embracing failure as a

learning opportunity, and fostering a culture of creativity and collaboration.

Inspirational Stories of Overcoming Challenges

1. Netflix: Netflix's transformation from a DVD rental service to a global streaming powerhouse is a testament to its ability to adapt and innovate in the face of adversity. Despite facing challenges such as technological disruption, content licensing negotiations, and competition from incumbents, Netflix has consistently reinvented itself and remained at the forefront of the entertainment industry.

2. Airbnb: Airbnb's journey from a struggling startup to a disruptor in the hospitality industry is a story of resilience, creativity, and perseverance. Despite facing regulatory hurdles, legal challenges, and skepticism from traditional industry players, Airbnb has leveraged technology and the sharing economy to create a global community of hosts and guests.

Key Takeaways

1. Innovation and Adaptability: Successful organizations are agile and adaptable, willing to embrace change and disrupt traditional paradigms to drive innovation and growth.

2. Customer-Centricity: Putting the customer at the center of business decisions is essential for building loyalty, driving satisfaction, and sustaining long-term success.

3. Resilience and Perseverance: Overcoming challenges and setbacks requires resilience, perseverance, and a willingness to learn from failure.

By studying case studies and success stories from industry leaders, organizations can gain valuable insights, inspiration, and actionable strategies for planning, executing, and overcoming challenges in their journey toward success.

XVIII. Action Plan and Implementation Guide:

Developing a personalized action plan and implementing it effectively are crucial steps toward achieving goals and objectives. This section creates an action plan and a step-by-step implementation guide:

Developing Your Personalized Action Plan

1. Goal Setting: Clearly define your goals, objectives, and desired outcomes. Ensure that they are specific, measurable, achievable, relevant, and time-bound (SMART).
2. Assessment of Current Situation: Evaluate your current situation, resources, strengths, weaknesses, opportunities, and threats (SWOT analysis). Identify any barriers or challenges that may hinder progress toward your goals.
3. Identifying Key Strategies and Tactics: Determine the strategies and tactics you will use to achieve your goals. Break

down your objectives into smaller, actionable steps and prioritize them based on their importance and feasibility.

4. Setting Milestones and Timelines: Establish milestones and timelines to track progress and maintain accountability. Break down your action plan into manageable phases or stages with clear deadlines for completion.

Step-by-Step Implementation Guide

1. Assign Responsibilities: Clearly define roles and responsibilities for each task or action item. Assign ownership to individuals or teams and communicate expectations, deadlines, and deliverables.
2. Allocate Resources: Ensure that adequate resources, including budget, manpower, and technology, are allocated to support the implementation of your action plan. Monitor resource utilization and adjust as needed to optimize efficiency.
3. Create an Execution Timeline: Develop a detailed timeline or project plan outlining

the sequence of activities, dependencies, and milestones. Use project management tools and techniques to track progress, identify bottlenecks, and mitigate risks.

4. Communication and Collaboration: Foster open communication and collaboration among team members to ensure alignment and coordination. Provide regular updates, share feedback, and address any issues or concerns that arise during implementation.

Tracking Progress and Adjusting Strategies

1. Monitoring and Evaluation: Implement mechanisms to monitor progress towards your goals and objectives. Track key performance indicators (KPIs), milestones, and metrics to assess progress and identify areas for improvement.

2. Regular Review and Reflection: Conduct regular reviews and reflections to evaluate the effectiveness of your action plan and implementation strategies. Identify successes, lessons learned, and opportunities for optimization.

3. Flexibility and Adaptability: Remain flexible and adaptable in response to changes in the internal or external environment. Be prepared to adjust strategies, reallocate resources, or pivot direction if necessary to stay on course toward your goals.
4. Continuous Improvement: Embrace a culture of continuous improvement by incorporating feedback, lessons learned, and best practices into your action plan. Iterate and refine your strategies based on insights gained from monitoring and evaluation.

By developing a personalized action plan, implementing it systematically, and tracking progress while remaining adaptable, organizations can effectively achieve their goals and drive success. A well-executed action plan serves as a roadmap for navigating challenges, seizing opportunities, and realizing desired outcomes.

XIX. Resources and Tools

Accessing reliable resources and utilizing effective tools are essential for enhancing knowledge, skills, and productivity in business planning and management. This section presents recommended resources and tools:

Recommended Books, Articles, and Websites

1. Books:
    - "The Lean Startup" by Eric Ries: Offers insights into lean methodologies and agile practices for building successful startups.
    - "Good to Great" by Jim Collins: Examines the factors that differentiate great companies from their competitors and offers actionable strategies for sustainable growth.
    - "The Innovator's Dilemma" by Clayton Christensen: Explores disruptive innovation and its implications for established businesses.

2. Articles and Websites:
    - Harvard Business Review (HBR): Provides thought-provoking articles, case studies, and insights on various business topics.
    - Forbes: Offers a wide range of articles, analyses, and expert opinions on business trends, entrepreneurship, and leadership.
    - Inc.: Features articles, interviews, and resources for startups and small businesses, covering topics such as growth strategies, management practices, and innovation.

Business Planning Templates and Checklists

1. Business Model Canvas: A visual tool for developing and refining business models, outlining key components such as value proposition, customer segments, revenue streams, and cost structure.
2. SWOT Analysis Template: Helps organizations assess strengths, weaknesses, opportunities, and threats to

inform strategic planning and decision-making.

3. Financial Planning Templates: Includes templates for creating financial projections, budgeting, cash flow statements, and balance sheets to support business planning and financial management.

4. Project Management Tools: Platforms such as Asana, Trello, and Monday.com offer customizable templates and checklists for project planning, task management, and collaboration.

Online Courses and Workshops

1. Coursera: Offers a wide range of online courses and specializations on business topics, including entrepreneurship, strategy, marketing, finance, and leadership.

2. Udemy: Provides affordable courses on business planning, management skills, startup growth strategies, and other relevant topics taught by industry experts.

3. LinkedIn Learning: Offers video tutorials and courses on business planning, project management, leadership development, and other professional skills.
4. Virtual Workshops and Webinars: Many organizations and industry associations host virtual workshops and webinars on business planning, entrepreneurship, and leadership development. Check event listings and professional networks for upcoming opportunities.

Key Benefits of Utilizing Resources and Tools

1. Knowledge Acquisition: Accessing recommended books, articles, and online courses enables individuals to deepen their understanding of business concepts, strategies, and best practices.
2. Efficiency and Effectiveness: Business planning templates, checklists, and project management tools streamline processes, improve organization, and enhance productivity.

3. Skill Development: Participating in online courses, workshops, and webinars helps individuals develop critical skills such as strategic thinking, decision-making, and communication.
4. Continuous Improvement: By leveraging resources and tools, individuals and organizations can stay informed, adapt to changing circumstances, and continuously improve their business planning and management practices.

By leveraging recommended resources and tools, individuals and organizations can enhance their knowledge, skills, and capabilities in business planning and management, driving success and achieving their goals effectively.

XX. Conclusion

As you embark on your business journey, it's essential to reflect on the key principles and strategies discussed throughout this guide and reinforce your commitment to achieving success. In conclusion, here are some final thoughts and words of encouragement:

Final Thoughts on Achieving Business Success

1. Vision and Purpose: Clarify your vision, define your purpose, and set ambitious yet achievable goals that align with your values and aspirations.
2. Strategy and Execution: Develop a robust business strategy and execution plan, focusing on innovation, differentiation, and value creation to drive sustainable growth and success.
3. Resilience and Adaptability: Embrace resilience and adaptability as essential qualities for navigating

4. challenges, overcoming obstacles, and seizing opportunities in an ever-changing business landscape.

Encouragement for Continuous Improvement and Growth

1. Lifelong Learning: Commit to continuous learning and personal growth, seeking out new knowledge, skills, and experiences that will enable you to evolve and thrive in your business endeavors.
2. Innovation and Creativity: Cultivate a culture of innovation and creativity within your organization, encouraging experimentation, exploration, and bold ideas that push the boundaries of what's possible.
3. Collaboration and Support: Surround yourself with a strong network of mentors, advisors, and peers who can offer guidance, support, and inspiration on your entrepreneurial journey.

Thank You and Best Wishes on Your Business Journey

As you embark on this exciting adventure of entrepreneurship and business ownership, I want to extend my sincere gratitude for your dedication, passion, and commitment to building a successful enterprise. Remember that every challenge you face, every setback you encounter, and every milestone you achieve is an opportunity for growth and learning.

Thank you for entrusting me to guide you through this journey, and I wish you nothing but the best in all your future endeavors. May your business journey be filled with success, fulfillment, and prosperity.

www.ingramcontent.com/pod-product-compliance
Lightning Source LLC
Chambersburg PA
CBHW071057290526
45795CB00004B/1535